SEA MONSTERS

CHRISTOPHER BAHN

CREATIVE EDUCATION • CREATIVE PAPERBACKS

Published by Creative Education and Creative Paperbacks
P.O. Box 227, Mankato, Minnesota 56002
Creative Education and Creative Paperbacks
are imprints of The Creative Company
www.thecreativecompany.us

Design by Graham Morgan
Art direction by Blue Design (www.bluedes.com)

Images by Alamy Stock Photo/Amanda Cotton, 12, Chronicle, 22, David Shale, 39, dieKleinert, 26, Jeff Rotman, 40, Jerry LoFaro/Stocktrek Images, 2; Getty Images/ Bettmann, 44, MR1805, 33, Racksuz, 28, Vaara, 24; Microsoft Designer/AI Generated, cover, 1; Shutterstock/ best works, 41, ChastityQ, 30, Herschel Hoffmeyer, 34, Melkor3D, 6, 35, OSORIOartist, 31, Sergei Proshchenko, 36; Unsplash/Conrad Ziebland, 11, Joel Bengs, 4–5; Wikimedia Commons/Alphonse-Marie-Adolphe de Neuville & Henri Théophile Hildibrand, 8, Bajirao1007, 13, Carole Raddato, 19, D. Gordon E. Robertson, 17, Lorenz Frølich, 18, Oilshale, 32, Pavel.Riha.CB, 3, Public Domain, 14, 15, 20, 25, 42, Thomas Bartholin, 16, William Frederick Mitchell, 43

Every effort has been made to contact copyright holders for material reproduced in this book. Any omissions will be rectified in subsequent printings if notice is given to the publisher.

Copyright © 2025 Creative Education, Creative Paperbacks
International copyright reserved in all countries.
No part of this book may be reproduced in any form
without written permission from the publisher.

Library of Congress Cataloging-in-Publication Data
Names: Bahn, Christopher (Children's story writer), author.
Title: Sea monsters / Christopher Bahn.
Description: Mankato, Minnesota : Creative Education and Creative Paperbacks, [2025] | Series: Enduring mysteries | Includes bibliographical references and index. | Audience: Ages 10–14 | Audience: Grades 7–9 | Summary: "An investigative approach to the mystery surrounding sea monsters for age 12 and up, from historical accounts and popular myths to hard facts and evidence. Includes a glossary, index, sidebars, and further resources"—Provided by publisher.
Identifiers: LCCN 2024015978 (print) | LCCN 2024015979 (ebook) | ISBN 9798889892892 (library binding) | ISBN 9781682776551 (paperback) | ISBN 9798889894001 (ebook)
Subjects: LCSH: Sea monsters—Juvenile literature. | Water—Folklore—Juvenile literature.
Classification: LCC QL89.2.S4 B35 2025 (print) | LCC QL89.2.S4 (ebook) | DDC 001.944—dc23/eng/20240409
LC record available at https://lccn.loc.gov/2024015978
LC ebook record available at https://lccn.loc.gov/2024015979

Printed in China

CONTENTS

Introduction 9

Spirits of the Deep 10

Real Beasts Below 21

Sea Monster Culture 29

Exploring the Ocean 37

Field Notes 46

Selected Bibliography 47

Websites 47

Index 48

INTRODUCTION

OPPOSITE: Captain Nemo takes an axe to a sea monster's tentacle in a scene from Jules Verne's 1870 novel.

T he great submarine *Nautilus* moves swiftly through the deep, dark sea. Suddenly, through the observation port, the passengers see a gigantic creature overtake the vessel and latch on with its eight massive tentacles, each equipped with hundreds of suckers. The ship grinds to a halt, jarring the crew members inside. Captain Nemo grimly announces that the beast has jammed its enormous, horned beak into the sub's propeller. The crew will have to fight it on the surface.

The men grab axes and a harpoon and climb the ladder to the top hatch. The sea creature slides one of its suckered arms through the opening, followed by 20 more. At least a dozen deadly squid are attacking the ship. A sailor is seized by one of the whiplike tentacles and cries out for help. With frantic sweeps of their axes, crew members lop off many of the monster's tentacles. But the creature shoots a black liquid at them and escapes, dragging the screaming sailor away. The remaining squid swarm the deck and are kept at bay only through a brave, desperate defense by Nemo and his men. At last, the creatures vanish back beneath the waves.

This scene is from Jules Verne's classic novel *Twenty Thousand Leagues under the Sea*. It may be fictional, but sea monsters such as these—and the real animals they are based on—have inspired both dread and wonder for thousands of years.

SPIRITS OF THE DEEP

OPPOSITE: The open ocean holds many secrets, including possible monsters, beneath its surface.

The Ocean has its silent caves,
Deep, quiet, and alone;
Though there be fury on the waves,
Beneath them there is none.
The awful spirits of the deep
Hold their communion there;
And there are those for whom we weep,
The young, the bright, the fair.

Those are the words of American writer Nathaniel Hawthorne (1804–64) in his poem "The Ocean," talking about humanity's **ambivalent** relationship with the sea. Since before the dawn of civilization, the ocean has brought people both endless dreams and boundless nightmares. It is a source of life but also a deep abyss of mystery that keeps secrets in a darkness

that has never seen the light of the sun. The profound vastness and unknowability of the sea have inspired many myths and stories around the world. And the glimpses people have had of the creatures that live there—whales, sharks, giant squid, and all manner of strange and unusual fish—have inspired further wonder: *What else might be down there, lurking?*

All life on Earth comes from the ocean, where the first organisms evolved billions of years ago. It is the largest habitat on the planet. More than 95 percent of the living space on Earth is in the ocean, and up to 80 percent of all living things are still found there. But humans have explored only 5 percent of the world's seas.

People have been living on and exploring the ocean for many thousands of years. Ancient Australians sailed it 40,000 years ago

OPPOSITE: Squid have a distinct and unique appearance, which makes them a common choice for monster stories.

to reach the southern continent. The Polynesian settlement of the Pacific Ocean stands as one of humanity's greatest achievements of exploration. Sailors navigated thousands of miles of open ocean, despite Stone Age technology, with astonishing insight and bravery.

In Europe, sailing vessels connected far-flung lands through trade going back at least 5,000 years. It's little wonder that tales of sea monsters are that old as well. "Undoubtedly, seafaring folk did witness giant creatures in the seas and oceans of the world, and many were hitherto unknown species," writes researcher Paul Harrison in his book *Sea Serpents and Lake Monsters of the British Isles*. "Those who encountered the whale for the first time could be forgiven for misinterpreting it as a nemesis of evil, surfacing from the deep to wreak carnage and devastation upon civilization as we know it."

THE GOD VISHNU

I n one of the ancient Hindu creation myths of India, the god Vishnu called forth the oceans and then rested, floating, on top of a serpent called Ananta Shesha. The leader of a group of snake-human hybrids called nagas, Ananta Shesha was said to have 5, 7, or even 1,000 heads—or more. It was strong enough to destroy an entire mountain. It also had power over storms, cast lightning from its mouth, and brought cool, pleasant rains.

RIGHT: Ancient Egyptians feared the snakelike god Apep, who was also known as "the evil lizard."

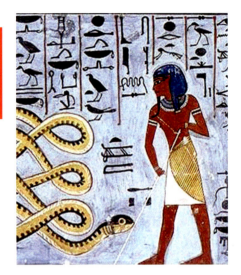

The Egyptian god Apep was a giant sea serpent that lived to spread destruction and chaos. He was a sworn enemy of the sun god, Ra. Apep lurked in the sea near the horizon and tried to stop Ra from completing his journey across the sky each day. Their conflict was represented in each day's fiery sunset. In Egyptian mythology, this story explained why day and night existed. Apep was also blamed for solar eclipses and storms.

In Mesopotamia, the ancient heart of what is now the Middle East, a similar sea serpent emerged. Its name was Labbu. Its body was 300 miles (483 kilometers) long. Labbu had a nasty habit of crawling ashore and eating people. Even the gods were terrified of Labbu and refused to fight it, said one myth. But it was slain at last by the storm god, Enlil, who raised a cloud against the creature.

The Greek poet Homer wrote his *Odyssey* around 700 B.C.E. In it, Odysseus encounters many dangers on his sailing voyage back to Greece. In one adventure, he is forced to make a terrible choice. To get through a narrow passage, he has to slip his ship between Scylla, the six-headed monster, and Charybdis, the whirlpool. Scylla's role, in the words of the goddess Circe, is "to plague mankind." Odysseus knows that if he sails too close to Scylla, she will snare one sailor with each of her heads. But Charybdis will surely destroy his entire ship. As Odysseus and his men focus on avoiding the whirlpool, Scylla grabs and devours six of the strongest

SCULPTURE OF A GREEK SEA MONSTER

15

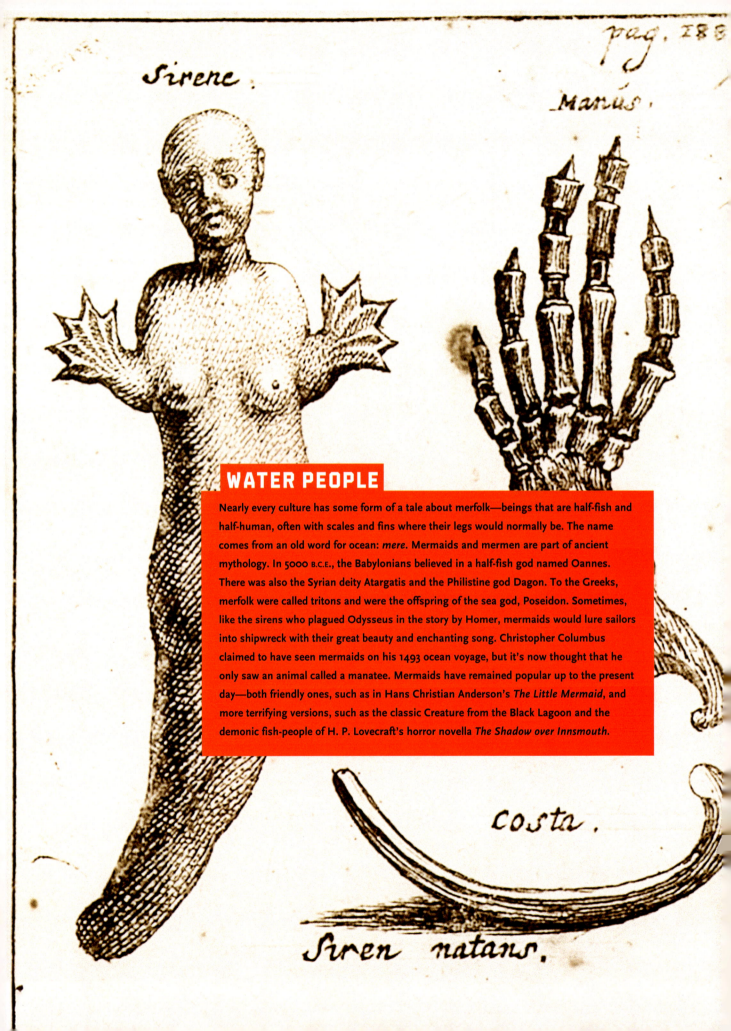

WATER PEOPLE

Nearly every culture has some form of a tale about merfolk—beings that are half-fish and half-human, often with scales and fins where their legs would normally be. The name comes from an old word for ocean: *mere*. Mermaids and mermen are part of ancient mythology. In 5000 B.C.E., the Babylonians believed in a half-fish god named Oannes. There was also the Syrian deity Atargatis and the Philistine god Dagon. To the Greeks, merfolk were called tritons and were the offspring of the sea god, Poseidon. Sometimes, like the sirens who plagued Odysseus in the story by Homer, mermaids would lure sailors into shipwreck with their great beauty and enchanting song. Christopher Columbus claimed to have seen mermaids on his 1493 ocean voyage, but it's now thought that he only saw an animal called a manatee. Mermaids have remained popular up to the present day—both friendly ones, such as in Hans Christian Anderson's *The Little Mermaid*, and more terrifying versions, such as the classic Creature from the Black Lagoon and the demonic fish-people of H. P. Lovecraft's horror novella *The Shadow over Innsmouth*.

ROCK WALL PAINTING OF MISHIPESHU

crew members. Odysseus can do nothing, but he and his surviving crew get through the passage.

In Chinese mythology, Gonggong was a water demon with a serpent's body and the head of a man with red hair. He battled Zhurong, the god of fire, and lost, but in his anger, he smashed a mountain that was holding up the sky. This caused everything on Earth to tilt to the west, which is why, says the myth, all of China's rivers flow east.

The Ojibwe of the Great Lakes of North America told of a fearsome water god called Mishipeshu who combined features of a lynx, a dragon, and a water serpent. Mishipeshu held power over the weather and waves, drowning many people in whirlpools, rapids, and ice storms. Its scales and horns were made of pure copper, and it was believed to be the guardian of this precious metal. Though terrifying, it would also bless people with gifts of medicine and safe passage across the lakes.

THOR BATTLES JÖRMUNGANDR

The Māori of New Zealand have tales of giant supernatural beings called taniwha. The creatures look like huge whales or sharks when at sea, but they can also tunnel under rivers or land, creating new harbors. If treated with respect, they protect humans.

In Japanese folktales, fishermen are terrorized by a monstrous sea-ghost called an umibōzu ("sea monk")—so named for its enormous bald head. In one story, it threatens to smash a fishing vessel unless the crew answers the question, "Name the most horrible thing you know!" One of the fishermen yells back, "My job!" Satisfied with the reply, the umibōzu disappears.

In Norse mythology, the Midgard Serpent, also called Jörmungandr, was so large that it encircled the entire world and bit its own tail. It is fated to fight the thunder god, Thor, in a battle to the death at the end of the world.

The aspidochelone was a massive turtle so large that Greek sailors would sometimes mistake it for an island. They discovered their error when they started a cooking fire on what they thought was a beach. The giant beast roared in pain and submerged, dragging the poor sailors to their watery deaths.

There are many more sea monster stories from around the globe. With advances in navigation around the year 1500, more and more ships began to travel across the open ocean during the period of history known as the Age of Sail. Sailors encountered more of the creatures that lived in the deep sea, and stories about the beasts began to trickle back to people on land. The stories were full of misunderstandings, half-truths, and outright exaggeration, probably mixing in details about multiple real animals. It would take some time for scientists to catch up to the fables. Either way, they made great stories.

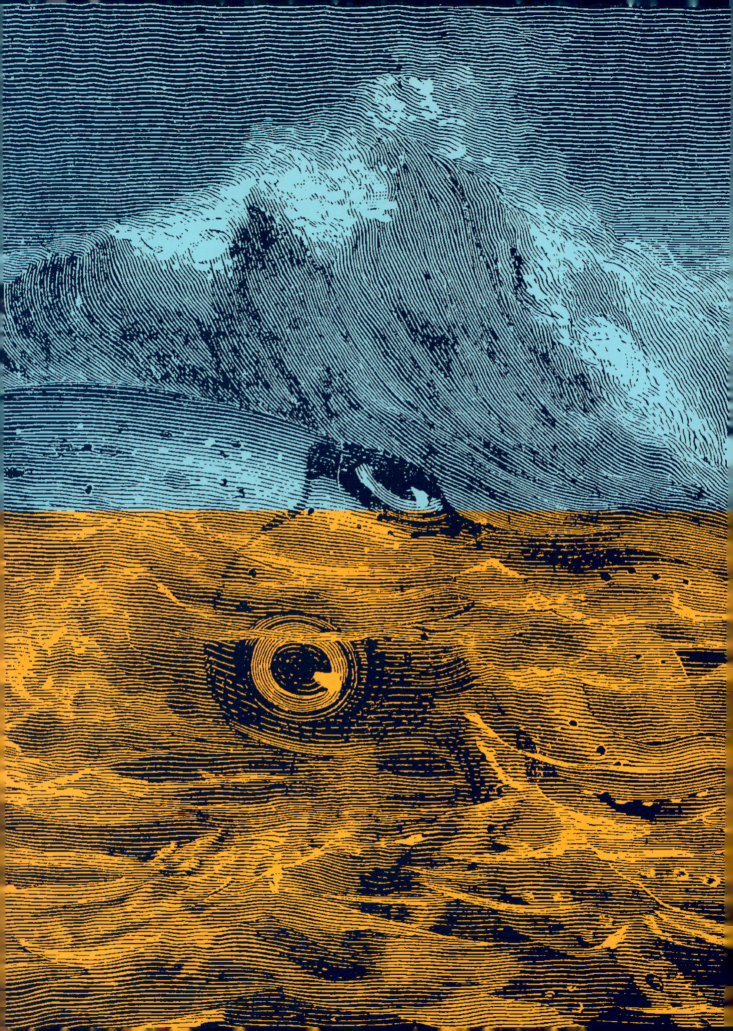

REAL BEASTS BELOW

Sea monster lore got a huge boost in the 16th and 18th centuries, thanks to two Scandinavian historians. The first was Olaus Magnus (1490–1557), a mapmaker and Catholic archbishop of Sweden. He created a map of the world's oceans in 1539 known as the *Carta Marina*. The map was filled with monsters and dangers of all kinds. In 1555, he described one as having a square head "all set with prickles," with long, sharp horns thick as tree trunks. Its huge eyes were "red and fiery-colored, which in the dark night appears as a burning fire. One of these sea monsters will drown easily many great ships." His accounts were frequently copied and became the basis for much of the modern mythology of sea monsters.

Two hundred years later, in 1753, Danish bishop Erik Pontoppidan built on Magnus's work in his book *A Natural History of Norway*. Pontoppidan was also a prominent scientist of his day, so his

OPPOSITE: Long-ago sightings of sea monsters with huge eyes are today attributed to giant squid or octopuses.

HERE BE DRAGONS

Early European mapmakers loved to decorate their maps with monsters. They did so partly as a warning of dangers and partly to fill in space that would otherwise be blank. One of the first three-dimensional globes showing the entire planet was the Lenox Globe, created around 1510. It included a phrase that has become famous as a warning for explorers of the dark unknown: "HIC SUNT DRACONES" ("HERE BE DRAGONS"). Sea monsters found on early maps included sea-elephants, mermaids gazing at themselves in mirrors, and violin-playing ichthyocentaurs (creatures that were part human, part horse, and part fish). According to historian Chet Van Duzer, most of these monsters weren't meant to be playful. They were based on the best science the mapmakers had available to them. Olaus Magnus's 1539 world map known as the *Carta Marina* features dozens of strange sea-beasts. It includes a violent whirlpool pulling a ship down to the depths, toothy creatures battling giant lobsters, and, worst of all, a giant red serpent 200 to 300 feet (61–91 m) long, wrapping itself around a ship and crushing it. Magnus insisted these creatures were real and a danger to travelers.

descriptions of giant sea serpents and other creatures were widely believed and spread worldwide. Although Pontoppidan was considered a painstaking collector of folklore and scientific information, later writers criticized him for being too quick to believe tall tales. He wrote about sea serpents more than 600 feet (182 meters) long, as well as mermaids.

Pontoppidan's most impressive find was the kraken, which he called the largest sea monster in the world. He described it as "round, flat, and full of arms" and more than 1.5 miles (2.4 km) around—big enough to be mistaken for several small islands. Although he thought kraken were not destructive by nature, he said that their sheer, mind-boggling size could threaten ships simply by rising up from the water and then diving again, creating a whirlpool that dragged ships along with it.

The idea that octopuses or squid were large and aggressive enough to attack ships was a popular notion among scientists of the 18th century, particularly French naturalist Pierre Denys de Montfort. His tales of "immense and malevolent octopuses" brought him ridicule and destroyed his career, though, when he claimed that 10 missing British warships had been sunk by angry cephalopods in 1782. They'd really just been lost in a hurricane.

As scientific knowledge progressed in the 19th century, biologists such as Richard Owen and Thomas Henry Huxley began to believe that the most outlandish sea monster stories must be exaggerations, although it was definitely true that giants such as whales and squid did exist. Those real sea creatures were certainly interesting in their own right—and even downright bizarre, sometimes. But the kind of sea monster found in fables was increasingly seen as unlikely, although there were some intriguing sightings. In 1848, the crew of the ship *Daedalus* claimed to have witnessed a snakelike creature at least 60 feet (18 m) long, brown

OPPOSITE: Illustrations from the 1700s often depicted sea serpents with mouthfuls of razor-sharp teeth.

and yellow in color, with a horselike head. And in 1914, during World War I (1914–18), a British steamship called the *Iberian* was sunk by a torpedo—and the explosion also, supposedly, killed a giant crocodile-like beast nearby, which was launched into the air by the blast.

The search for sea monsters in the 20th century increasingly turned to **cryptozoology** and writers such as Bernard Heuvelmans. Heuvelmans (1916–2001) was a Belgian-French scientist who earned a **doctorate** in zoology, the study of animals. But he gained his greatest fame from his research on **cryptids**. Today, Heuvelmans is considered a founder of the field of cryptozoology (a term he himself coined), which seeks to find and explain cryptid animals such as Bigfoot and the Loch Ness Monster. In 1982, he cofounded the International Society of Cryptozoology, which promoted the study of mystery animals. The group disbanded in 1998.

Most mainstream scientists consider cryptozoology to be a **pseudoscience** that lacks true scientific rigor. Heuvelmans, though, diligently cataloged thousands of reports of cryptids of all kinds. He also wrote several influential books, including the 1955 bestseller *On the Track of Unknown Animals* and his book on sea monsters, *In the Wake of the Sea Serpents,* which was published in French in 1965 and translated into English in 1968. In this book, Heuvelmans examined hundreds of sightings and declared that out in the oceans awaiting discovery were nine types of sea monster: long-necked, merhorse, many-humped, many-finned, super-otter, super-eel, marine saurian, father-of-all-the-turtles, and yellow belly.

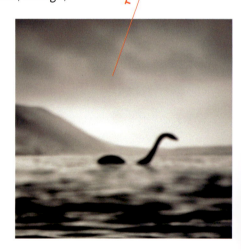

THE LOCH NESS MONSTER

Heuvelmans's approach was influential on many later cryptozoologists, who expanded on his classifications. But it hasn't been embraced by mainstream science. Darren Naish, a British **paleontologist** and the author of *Hunting Monsters: Cryptozoology and the Reality Behind the Myths*, calls *In the Wake of the Sea Serpents* "the most influential book ever written on sea monsters." But Naish also says Heuvelmans's system falls apart if investigated too closely. He adds that Heuvelmans was inconsistent and "sometimes duped by misidentifications and **hoaxes**." For example, the story of the *Iberian*, which Heuvelmans accepted uncritically, has been dismissed as an invention by later writers.

Many of the most grotesque and amazing sea monsters are not cryptids at all. They are real animals kept secret for centuries by the ocean's great depths. The kraken is largely based on the giant squid, which can reach sizes of 33 feet (10 m) or more. Its 10 tentacles are lined with hundreds of suckers like suction cups, which it uses to seize its prey and draw it into its parrotlike beak. Like an octopus, a giant squid can change color instantly to match its surroundings. The colossal squid is even larger, perhaps 1,500 pounds (700 kilograms) and 46 feet (14 m) in length. Its eye is the largest known of any animal—bigger than a basketball! Both kinds of squid are hunted by sperm whales, whose skin is often crisscrossed by

REAL BEASTS BELOW

25

OPPOSITE: The mythical kraken, based on the giant squid, battles a mighty sperm whale.

deep scars from battling squid. Although they range worldwide, giant squid are rarely encountered by humans, in part because they like to live in the deep, cold waters lying 980 to 3,280 feet (300–1,000 m) below the surface. No giant squid was caught on video underwater until 2012.

Squid and their relatives, the octopuses, are known as cephalopods. There are many different kinds. Octopuses are very intelligent, but their biology makes them seem like aliens. Boneless, they can squeeze through tiny openings. Unlike most animals, their blood is not iron-based and red. It's copper-based and blue. Like giant squid, they can change color and texture instantly. They can make themselves look like rocks or plants. Perhaps most weirdly, two-thirds of their nerve cells, responsible for sending signals to and from the brain, are located not in their brains but in their eight tentacles, which can sense and react independently.

Many reports of sea serpents were probably the giant oarfish, rarely seen above its preferred depth of 3,300 feet (1,000 m). Unlike Jörmungandr, the oarfish does not get big enough to encircle Earth. But it is the longest bony fish in the world. It can grow to more than 56 feet (17 m). A comblike red fin runs the length of its back.

Whales have inspired sea monster tales since ancient times, and it's easy to see why. They are simply huge. Blue whales, measuring 98 feet (30 m) and weighing up to 300,000 pounds (136,000 kg), are the biggest animals ever to appear on Earth. Sperm whales are the loudest animals in the world, making clicks that reach 230 decibels—louder than a jet engine.

SEA MONSTER CULTURE

OPPOSITE: The giant sea reptile called Mosasaurus lived until about 60 million years ago.

Life began in the sea, and over hundreds of millions of years, a dizzying array of creatures have swum though the waters. Many have since gone **extinct**, but paleontologists have been able to find evidence of some impressive specimens. Megalodon was an immense prehistoric shark that reached up to 67 feet (20 m) long, three times bigger than a great white. Archelon was a sea turtle 15 feet (4.5 m) long, the length of a modern minivan. Ancient whales included Livyatan and Basilosaurus, two giant predators with bone-crushing bites.

In the age of dinosaurs, the seas were ruled by reptiles such as Tylosaurus and Mosasaurus (memorably seen in the movie *Jurassic World*), which reached up to 56 feet (17 m) long. Their relatives, the plesiosaurs, had long necks and barrel-like, four-flippered bodies—like "a snake strung through the body of a turtle," in the words of English scientist William Buckland. Paleontologist Darren Naish suggests that

29

OPPOSITE: The Loch Ness Monster is described as having a shape similar to prehistoric plesiosaurs.

the popularity of plesiosaurs in the 1930s probably changed sea monster folklore—people stopped reporting that they'd seen sea serpents, in favor of plesiosaur-esque animals, and cryptozoologists began to openly wonder if plesiosaurs might have lived up to the present day.

While monsters of the open ocean are often terrifying and strange, lake monsters have a tendency to be seen as beloved mascots of their region. They may not exactly be cuddly, but they're from the neighborhood—and they help attract tourists, too. The most famous of the lake monsters is certainly Nessie, the legendary creature from Loch Ness in northern Scotland. Fed by **peat**-filled streams, the lake's deep, cold water is brown and murky—a perfect place for a water monster to hide, some say. Most commonly, witnesses say Nessie is a big, streamlined beast, with a small head on a long, thin neck—like a plesiosaur or sauropod dinosaur. Loch Ness Monster tales go back to the sixth century B.C.E., when an Irish missionary named St. Columba ordered a monster to stop attacking a swimmer. Nessie became known worldwide in 1933 when a burst of sightings and photographs were published. Some were later found to be hoaxes, but the legend lives on. Loch Ness attracts about one million visitors every year.

Dozens of similar monsters are said to be living in bodies of water around the world. "Chessie," a snakelike monster reportedly dwelling in Chesapeake Bay, has become a popular mascot for environmental groups' anti-pollution messages. People on two of Wisconsin's most popular recreational lakes, Geneva and Delavan, have seen monsters sticking their long necks above the water for more than a century. Canada's version of Nessie is known as Ogopogo. According to legend, Ogopogo lives in Lake

SECRET FISH

Despite today's advanced technology, it is difficult to explore the ocean, which is huge, dark, and dangerous. It's no wonder scientists keep finding new, amazing creatures. The coelacanth and the megamouth shark are two examples. The coelacanth is a large, bony fish that first appeared on Earth more than 400 million years ago. Scientists believed it had gone extinct 66 million years ago. But in 1938, living specimens were discovered off the coast of Africa, thriving in the depths and remaining essentially unchanged from their ancient ancestors. Coelacanths can be 6.5 feet (2 m) long and weigh nearly 200 pounds (91 kg). They live in caves deep below the surface and emerge to feed at night. The megamouth shark, which can be 18 feet (5.5 m) long and weigh 2,700 pounds (1,215 kg), had never been seen until one became entangled with the anchor of a U.S. Navy ship near Hawaii in 1976. Since then, about 100 megamouths have been seen or caught. They dive as deep as 15,000 feet (4,600 m). Considering the vast size of the ocean, it is almost certain that other unknown life-forms have yet to be discovered.

ALLEGED LAKE MONSTER

Okanagan, a 69-mile-long (111-km), 3-mile-wide (4.8-km), 750-foot-deep (229-m) lake in British Columbia. Ogopogo is said to have special powers and is even credited with the ability to control the weather. Unlike the gods of old, who unleashed rain and lightning but were never seen, Ogopogo has been sighted—as recently as 2019. Lake Champlain, a large freshwater body of water tucked among the farms and forests of Vermont and upstate New York, has its own monster. In 1870, steamship passengers on the lake reported seeing a beast in the water moving as fast as a train. In 1873, circus promoter P. T. Barnum offered a reward of $50,000 for its capture—dead or alive. Today the monster is known as "Champ," a friendly sea creature. It is even the mascot of the Futures Collegiate Baseball League team in Burlington, Vermont.

Perhaps the best place to find sea monsters is in fiction. The scaly, tentacled beasts have inspired classic poems, books, and movies for hundreds of years. In 1830, the English poet Alfred, Lord Tennyson, wrote "The Kraken," about a sleeping giant who lurks "below the thunders of the upper deep, far, far beneath in the abysmal sea." The creature will wake only, Tennyson implies, at the end of the world, when "in roaring he shall rise and on the surface die." J. R. R. Tolkien's *Fellowship of the Ring* fought against an octopoid, a many-tentacled monster known only as the Watcher in the Water. French novelist Victor Hugo, in 1866's *Toilers of the Sea*, pits his hero in a battle to the death with an octopus, which he memorably describes as "a glutinous mass, endowed with a malignant will—what can be more horrible?" Four years later, Jules Verne's Captain Nemo faced off against a swarm

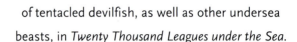

of tentacled devilfish, as well as other undersea beasts, in *Twenty Thousand Leagues under the Sea*. The giant squid in the 1954 Disney adaptation was frightful enough that the movie won that year's Academy Award for special effects. A kraken famously appears in the 1981 fantasy film *Clash of the Titans*, although this version is a four-armed giant rather than the octopuslike creature as commonly described. A more true-to-mythology kraken threatens Captain Jack Sparrow in *Pirates of the Caribbean: Dead Man's Chest*.

One of the most enduring fictional sea monsters is Cthulhu (KLUL-hloo), invented by the American horror writer H. P. Lovecraft in his 1928 short story "The Call of Cthulhu." A massive winged being hundreds of feet tall, Cthulhu resembles a strange hybrid dragon/octopus, with long tentacles hanging from where a face should be. Many authors have spun tales about Cthulhu, who has also made frequent appearances in modern video and board games.

The shark in the 1975 movie *Jaws* made people jump out of their seats when it flung itself onto the boat of its pursuers. Dozens of movies with sharks as villains followed, enhancing their fearsome image. In the 1999 film *Deep Blue Sea*, scientists enhance sharks' intelligence, making them more vicious killers than they are in nature. The 2013 movie *Sharknado* put killer sharks inside tornadoes—scary, if hardly realistic. In 2018, *The Meg* starred a 75-foot-long (23-m) megalodon.

Whales were pictured as fierce monsters in the 19th century, the heyday of whaling. They were often shown biting boats in half and ramming ships. Captain Ahab, in Herman Melville's 1851 novel *Moby-Dick*, went mad with obsession in his quest to find the great white whale that had bitten off his leg. In the end, the whale dragged Ahab down into the sea with him. A 1977 movie, *Orca*, involved a vengeful killer whale.

An imagining of Cthulhu

If there's one fictional sea-dwelling giant who has had the greatest cultural impact, however, it is Japan's king of the monsters, Godzilla. Godzilla is a massive, tyrannosaurlike beast as tall as a skyscraper. Armed with a dragonlike blast of atomic fire, he is nearly unstoppable. In his first movie appearance, in 1954, he was awakened from centuries of deep-ocean sleep by American nuclear-weapons tests. The effects of these tests changed the beast and sent him on a path of destruction across Japan's largest city, Tokyo. Godzilla's creators were inspired by the giant monsters from two earlier movies, *King Kong* and *The Beast from 20,000 Fathoms*. But Godzilla was also born as a comment on the dangers of nuclear weaponry, which was still fresh in the minds of the people of Japan (less than 10 years before, atomic bombs had destroyed two Japanese cities at the end of World War II [1939–45]). Since then, Godzilla has starred in nearly 40 movies. He has been reinvented several times—sometimes as a city-destroying villain and sometimes as humanity's protector against other giant monsters. The 2023 film *Godzilla Minus One* won an Academy Award for visual efffects.

SEA MONSTER CULTURE

EXPLORING THE OCEAN

Very little of the ocean has been thoroughly explored, but new advances are being made every year. The ocean is a single, unfathomably enormous system of water that spans the entire world. It's divided into five smaller oceans: Pacific, Atlantic, Indian, Southern/Antarctic, and Arctic. Scientists divide the ocean vertically into several zones based on the physical conditions and kinds of life found there.

The epipelagic zone is the topmost zone. It reaches down from the surface to 660 feet (200 m). Light from the sun penetrates deeply enough in this region that plants can grow. Because it's warmer and can support a wider variety of ecosystems than the deeper zones, most marine life is found in the epipelagic zone. The crushing weight of the water makes the pressure at the bottom of this zone 20 times greater than the air on the surface. The pressure is far too great for humans to survive without special equipment—and it gets much worse farther down.

OPPOSITE: Underwater researchers continue to discover new species of fish and other sea creatures.

OPPOSITE: The deep-sea anglerfish hunts prey in the dark bathypelagic zone.

The mesopelagic is the next zone. It extends from 660 to 3,300 feet (200–1,000 m) and is called the "twilight zone" because the light becomes very dim. It's also cold—about 39 degrees Fahrenheit (4 degrees Celsius) at the lowest point. The pressure is nearly 100 times greater than at the surface. Animals living in this zone (and deeper down) are often bioluminescent, which means they can make their own light. The mesopelagic zone is where giant squid roam and where the coelacanth was rediscovered in 1938. Other residents include poisonous pufferfish and cuttlefish. The most monstrous-sounding might be the vampire squid, which appears to wear a red cape that hides a set of eight arms lined with soft spikes. Its scientific name, *Vampyroteuthis infernalis*, translates as "vampire squid from hell." In fact, it's a passive food-gatherer, not a hunter.

The bathypelagic zone is the beginning of total darkness. No light can penetrate this much water. The "midnight zone" extends from 3,300 to 13,000 feet (1,000–4,000 m). Many animals here have very weak eyes or none at all. In 2017, a team of researchers working in deep water off eastern Australia discovered hundreds of previously unknown species in the bathypelagic zone. One of their finds was the terrifying deepsea lizardfish. The pale-bodied, big-eyed fish, which can grow more than 2 feet (0.6 m) long, doesn't find much food this far below the surface. It compensates by aggressively devouring anything it encounters, including other lizardfish, with its mouthful of jagged, sharp teeth.

The bathypelagic zone is an alien environment that's unexpectedly rich with life. **Hydrothermal vents** are found along undersea mountain ranges at an average depth of 7,000 feet (2,100 m). They constantly spew superheated, mineral-rich water. Despite temperatures of about

Submersibles allow scientists to explore—firsthand—parts of the ocean that were previously difficult to reach.

OCEAN DEPTHS EXCEED HEIGHTS ON LAND.

750 °F (400 °C), many animals thrive there, including bacteria, tubeworms, octopuses, and a bristly, snow-white **crustacean** called a yeti crab, so named for the Abominable Snowman.

The abyssopelagic zone, which starts at 13,000 feet (4,000 m) and drops down to 20,000 feet (6,000 m), covers a large part of the ocean floor. It is eerily quiet, and most animals here are tiny, to cope with the extraordinary pressure. But one crustacean—*Bathynomus giganteus*, which is related to woodlice—reaches the impressive size of 16 inches (41 centimeters).

Finally, the hadal zone, lying 20,000 to 36,200 feet (6,000–11,000 m) below the surface, includes the deepest parts of the ocean. The Challenger Deep is the lowest point of the Mariana Trench, between Japan and New Guinea. It has been estimated at 35,827 feet (10,920 m)—nearly 7 miles (11 km)—below the surface and 7,000 feet (2,133 m) deeper than Mount Everest is tall! Almost unbelievably, there is life down here. Scientists have found about 400 different species, including crustaceans, abyssal cusk-eels, and snailfish.

The darkness, cold, and water pressure make it hard for humans to get down this far, but it has been done. The world record for diving on a single breath, 831 feet (253 m), was set in 2012 by Austrian Herbert Nitsch. The **scuba**-diving depth record, 1,090 feet (332 m), was set by Egyptian Ahmed Gabr in 2014. Scuba diving deeper than 130 feet (40 m) is considered extremely risky because of the pressure of the water and the need to breathe gases other than oxygen. A naval submarine is believed to be able to drop safely to 1,600 feet (488 m).

EXPLORING THE OCEAN

TRIESTE

These depths might seem to limit how much underwater exploring people can do. But technology has created some new options. Small and tough **submersibles** carry people and equipment far deeper than they were able to go in the past. *Alvin*, a submersible built in 1964, explored the wreck of *Titanic* 12,500 feet (3,810 m) below the surface of the North Atlantic. It later dove to 14,800 feet (4,511 m).

The Mariana Trench is protected by the United States as the Marianas Trench Marine National Monument. There have been only a few descents to the bottom of the trench. The first was *Trieste*, owned by the U.S. Navy, in 1960. Two men were aboard. The next two crafts were unpiloted. One was the Japanese *Kaiko* in 1995. The other was *Nereus* in 2009. The next crewed descent was in 2012 in the *Deepsea Challenger*, piloted by *Titanic* film director James Cameron. And beginning in 2019, the deep-sea vessel *Limiting Factor* visited the trench repeatedly, bringing more than 20 scientists and explorers to this remote but fascinating place.

The National Oceanic and Atmospheric Administration (NOAA) is best known for keeping track of storms and other dangerous weather. But it also explores the depths of the sea. Its *Okeanos Explorer* is a

THE FIRST CHALLENGE

Scientists today who study the mysteries of the deep ocean are heirs to a tradition begun in 1872 by the HMS *Challenger*, a British Navy warship that became the world's first oceanic research vessel. The 225-foot (69-m) **corvette** was stripped of all but two of its guns. It was equipped with laboratories, extra cabins, scientific equipment, a dredging deck, and 181 miles (291 km) of rope for pulling up samples from the ocean below. It left Portsmouth, England, with a crew of 216, plus 21 officers and 6 scientists. For nearly 4 years, under both sail and steam, it circled the globe, covering 68,930 miles (110,932 km). It even traveled to Antarctica. Seafloor samples were collected, and scientists measured depths, temperatures, currents, and water chemistry. They discovered more than 4,700 plants and animals. The report on the results took 23 years to complete and filled 29,500 pages in 50 volumes! The voyage is regarded as the birth of oceanography, the scientific study of the ocean. It is known for finding the ocean's deepest spot: Challenger Deep, in the Mariana Trench.

224-foot (68-m) former navy ship launched in 2010 to conduct ocean research. The vessel has traveled the world. It maps the seafloor, tracks pollution, investigates undersea eruptions, and observes the animals living down below. To do that, it carries electronic equipment such as **sonar** and remotely operated vehicles (ROVs). Researchers on the ship use computers to guide ROVs through the sea to investigate things and places people can't access. The website of the *Okeanos Explorer* has an extensive photo collection of creatures, corals, and other items its researchers have encountered. It's called the Benthic Deepwater Animal Identification Guide.

As scientists have explored the deep sea, they have discovered many bizarre and seemingly unearthly animals. But no krakens, mermaids, or other legendary creatures have been found—at least, not yet. Should people keep hoping that sea monsters like that really exist? It's hard not to be doubtful. After all, it's now a fact that the most famous picture of the Loch Ness Monster was a hoax—a toy serpent's body attached to a toy submarine. But the ocean is still deep, dark, and mostly unexplored. Who knows what else is down there?

To John Steinbeck, one of the great American writers of the 20th century, sea monsters were not just the residents of the deep sea but the deep human mind. In his 1951 book *The Log from the Sea of Cortez*, Steinbeck called sea monsters "dream symbols" and said that if, someday, "a true sea-serpent, complete and undecayed, is found or caught, a shout of triumph will go through the world."

"Men really need sea monsters in their personal ocean," Steinbeck wrote. "An ocean without its unnamed monsters would be like a completely dreamless sleep."

FIELD NOTES

ambivalent—to have mixed feelings about something

corvette—a small, lightly armed but highly maneuverable warship

crustacean—a water creature, such as a lobster or crab, that has a hard outer shell

cryptid—an animal which some people think might be real but which has never been proven to be real, such as Bigfoot or the Loch Ness Monster

cryptozoology—the study of and search for evidence to prove the existence of legendary or extinct cryptid animals

doctorate—the highest level of academic degree

extinct—no longer existing; when said of a group of animals or plants, to have no living representatives

hoax—a humorous or harmful deception; a trick

hydrothermal vent—an opening in Earth's surface from which heated water emerges

paleontologist—a scientist who studies ancient animal and plant life

peat—brown, partially decayed plant material that can be dried and used for fuel

pseudoscience—beliefs or practices that are mistakenly or fraudulently thought to be based on solid scientific principles

scuba—a type of diving that uses special equipment to be able to breathe underwater

sonar—a technique using sound waves to navigate, find, or communicate with other objects underwater

submersible—a vessel that can work deep underwater

SELECTED BIBLIOGRAPHY

Costantino, Grace. "Five 'Real' Sea Monsters Brought to Life by Early Naturalists." *Smithsonian Magazine.* October 27, 2014. https://www.smithsonianmag.com/science-nature/five-real-sea-monsters-brought-life-early-naturalists-180953155.

Ellis, Richard. *The Search for the Giant Squid.* New York: Lyons Press, 1998.

Hoyt, Erich. *Creatures of the Deep: In Search of the Sea's Monsters and the World They Live In.* Buffalo, N.Y.: Firefly Books, 2021.

Loxton, Daniel, and Donald R. Prothero. *Abominable Science! Origins of the Yeti, Nessie, and Other Famous Cryptids.* New York: Columbia University Press, 2013.

Naish, Darren. *Ancient Sea Reptiles: Plesiosaurs, Ichthyosaurs, Mosasaurs, and More.* Washington, D.C.: Smithsonian Books, 2022.

Rose, Carol. *Giants, Monsters, and Dragons: An Encyclopedia of Folklore, Legend, and Myth.* Santa Barbara, Calif.: ABC-CLIO, 2000.

Van Duzer, Chet. *Sea Monsters on Medieval and Renaissance Maps.* London: The British Library, 2013.

WEBSITES

Giant Squid: June 20, 2019
https://oceanexplorer.noaa.gov/video_playlist/best_5_squid.html
Get up close to a real giant squid in this short deep-sea video.

Know Your Ocean
https://www.whoi.edu/know-your-ocean
Discover facts about Earth's oceans.

Sea Monsters
https://www.amnh.org/exhibitions/mythic-creatures/water-creatures-of-the-deep/sea-monsters
Learn the history behind a variety of sea monsters.

INDEX

Alfred, Lord Tennyson, 33
American Indian myths
    Mishipeshu, 17
Carta Marina, 21, 22
Challenger Deep, 41, 43
"Champ," 33
"Chessie," 30
Chinese myths
    Gonggong, 17
cryptids, 24, 25
cryptozoology, 24, 25, 30
Cthulhu, 34, 35
Denys de Montfort, Pierre, 23
Egyptian myths
    Apep, 14
fish, 12, 16, 22, 27, 32, 34, 37, 38, 41
Godzilla, 35
Greek myths
    Odysseus and Scylla, 14, 17
Harrison, Paul, 13
Hawthorne, Nathaniel, 10
Heuvelmans, Bernard, 24, 25
Hindu myths
    Ananta Shesha, 13
hoaxes, 25, 30, 45
Hugo, Victor, 33
Iberian, 24, 25
Japanese myths
    umibōzu ("sea monk"), 18
kraken, 21, 23, 25, 27, 34
lakes, 17, 30, 33
Loch Ness Monster ("Nessie"), 24, 30, 45
Lovecraft, H. P., 34
Magnus, Olaus, 21
Māori myths
    taniwha, 18
Mariana Trench, 42, 43
merfolk, 16, 23, 45
Mesopotamian myths
    Labbu, 14
Mosasaurus, 29
Naish, Darren, 25, 29

Norse myths
    Jörmungandr, 18, 27
    Midgard Serpent. *See* Jörmungandr
oarfish, 27
octopuses, 21, 23, 25, 27, 33, 34, 41
Ogopogo, 30, 33
plesiosaurs, 29–30
Pontoppidan, Erik, 21, 23
research vessels
    HMS *Challenger*, 43
    Okeanos Explorer, 42, 45
    submersibles, 40, 42
sharks, 12, 18, 29, 34
    Megalodon, 29, 34
squid, 9, 21, 23, 25, 27, 34, 38
Steinbeck, John, 45
tentacles, 9, 25, 27, 33, 34
Tolkien, J. R. R., 33–34
turtles, 18, 24, 29
    Archelon, 29
    aspidochelone, 18
Twenty Thousand Leagues under the Sea, 9, 34
Verne, Jules, 9, 33
whales, 12, 13, 18, 25, 27, 29, 34
    Moby-Dick, 34
zones of the ocean, 37–38, 41